Summers in France

Summers in France

Kathryn M. Ireland

GIBBS SMITH
TO ENRICH AND INSPIRE HUMANKIND

To my darlings,
Oscar, Otis
and Louis, who
put up with all
those summers
in France!

Table of Contents

Foreword

No one has ever stayed at Kathryn's **farmhouse** near **Toulouse** without wishing they **owned** something similar themselves. Deep in Cathar country, in one of the last properly rural areas of southwest France, she has created the alluring French idyll that exists deep inside all of us: the tumbledown farm brought glamorously back to life, fabulous food, sunshine, the laughter of friends.

And so many friends. You never know who you'll bump into next in the kitchen: it might be an Oscar-winning actress or a Manhattan restaurateur. Decorators and designers, society chefs, photographers, Shakespearean actors and East Coast fabric tycoons all gravitate to Kathryn's table with its ever-changing cast of characters. To be in her orbit is to be bathed in generosity, love-bombed with delicious food, gossip and warmth. Her French house is a sophisticated exercise in sustainable upscale bohemia, where the atmosphere is gloriously relaxed but everything somehow works perfectly.

Everything is on a big scale: a dozen or two dozen people for lunch and dinner every single day in the open-sided barn that serves as an outdoors dining room; huge squashy sofas everywhere, occupied by sprawling teenagers or children watching DVDs; giant ceramic and terracotta bowls filled with lemons from her trees; bolts of Provencal fabrics from her latest collections; a stable full of horses, and a major barbecue sizzling with grilled chicken and earthy Toulouse sausages. And at the centre of it all, Kathryn herself, often dressed in the sexy suede chaps of her riding kit, drawing everyone (quite literally) to her bosom and cackling with raspy laughter.

There is no fixed boundary between inside and outside: every door stands open to the garden and the numerous outside sitting areas of wicker chairs covered with cushions in her trademark fabrics. Children sleep on the lawns under duvets in the open air. In the fields around the house, sunflowers turn their faces 180 degrees during the course of the day, following the trajectory of the sun. Teenagers cluster by the swimming pool behind the pigeonnier on romantic assignations; guests of ages from four to seventy play fifteen-a-side football matches in the evening cool.

A local farmer arrives with jars of his homemade foie gras, which looks like body parts in formaldehyde but tastes wonderful. Each morning guests set off on shopping trips to the market, returning weighed down with sweet-smelling melons, beefsteak tomatoes and aubergines for another lunchtime feast.

If there is anywhere on earth more fun or more chic, I have not found it.

—Nicholas Coleridge
Managing Director, Condé Nast Britain

It's a **magical** place where ponies run wild through **fields** of sunflowers.

Introduction

On a whim one bleak midwinter February, pregnant with my first child, my nesting instincts urged me to take a trip through France with the unrealistic goal of finding and buying some rundown château. I had gone to California on a whim the year before and met and married the father of my three boys. Instantly, I had a new home—far from where I had grown up.

The idea of summers in France was a dream. I was working in London with my husband, Gary Weis, and it seemed crazy not to take a trip to France to look for a place where I could take my children for their summer holidays so they would have a sense of Europe growing up and would have wonderful memories of their childhood, as I did of mine.

Unbeknownst to my husband, I had scoured the *Herald Tribune*, the *Sunday Times*, and any magazine that listed houses for sale in France. I had calculated a trip throughout the west of France, through the Dordogne all the way to Provence in search of a house. Gary and I set out from our rental in Somerset, England, and took the ferry to Calais. We drove through Paris and spent a night close to Versailles, where we had the most unbelievable dinner and my first bottle of fizzy-less champagne. The following day we continued to the Dordogne and stayed at Sarlat—picturesque but a little Gothic for me. We visited a few houses but nothing that I had to have.

I always know what time of summer it is by the dispensation of the sunflowers. In early June they are just breaking ground, but by late July—early August, they are in full bloom.

I was map reader and, with the map of France spread out in front of me, it dawned on me as we were driving south on the A61 towards Toulouse that the area we were coming to next was the subject of a postcard sent to Gary the previous year from friends who had a house in one of the fortified medieval villages, Bruniquel. I leapt at the opportunity to explore this area instead of continuing on to Provence. In my handbag I had the name of a real estate agent that my father's accountant had given me; I called her from a pay phone in Cahors and asked if she had anything to show me. She did. Driving through the overcast countryside reminded me of my family's retreat in southwest Scotland. There was a perfect mélange of farmland and architecture that brought the two places I love the most together—Tuscany and the west coast of Scotland. I just knew this was where I wanted a house. I felt that a shepherd's croft, barn or chateau was waiting for my love and attention. We drove on— I with the intention to buy a house and Gary to have lunch.

We met the realtor in Monclar-de-Quercy, a somewhat sleepy little town with a very pretty square and an impressive early 19th-century *marie* (mayor's office). The agent told us we were going to see a rambling farmhouse with sixteen hectares.

As we came down the driveway, I had that same feeling I had had when I saw the Grand Canyon for the first time. The sweeping, uninterrupted views over the Tarn Valley facing south towards the Pyrénées were spectacular. The house sat on a knoll with 360-degree views. I knew instantly that the house and surrounding barns could become home.

—Kathryn M. Ireland
Interior & Textile Designer

1.
The Towns and Markets.

The Tarn-et-Garonne is a completely unspoiled region of France that lies equidistant from the Atlantic and Mediterranean.

Historically, it is one of the most important parts of Europe because of its proximity to the Spanish border. The countryside is littered with *bastides*, fortified towns perched on top of hills, originally built to defend the surrounding countryside from the oncoming enemy.

It wasn't just the house, but the people and the area's history were important to me. Where would we be having a cup of coffee, a slice of pizza? Who was the local farmer to buy produce from? These locals, after all, were to be my friends, the core of my existence.

This area was home of the Cathars, a twelfth-century religious group that, among other things, promoted feminism and equality for the serfs—and were vegetarians. Becoming a threat to Rome, most of them were rounded up and burned at the stake as "witches."

I mention this because one of my dear girlfriends, Donna Dixon Akyroyd, arranged for me to have my chakras read. The seer herself was taken aback when she told me that I had been a witch—not only once, but in three of my previous lives. I had, however, been a good witch, but burned at the stake nonetheless. Thinking this was a customary finding, I shrugged it off for a few minutes before asking for how many of her clients did this come up. To my amazement—none! She then assured me that witches were good, and, all of a sudden, I understood why I had bought a house 4,000 miles away in France when I lived in California! I felt like I was coming home.

The farm is in the Midi-Pyrénées, on the borders of the Tarn and the Tarn-et-Garonne, named after the two largest rivers in the area.

London
Channel
Brussels
Luxembourg
Paris
tlantic
Bordeaux
Monclar
Albi
Toulouse
Bilbao
N
E
S
Mediterrane
Barcelona

Medieval hilltop towns, rolling hills, Cathar History, open air produce markets where "biologique" is a given.

There really aren't any rules here, just boundaries that the children respect.

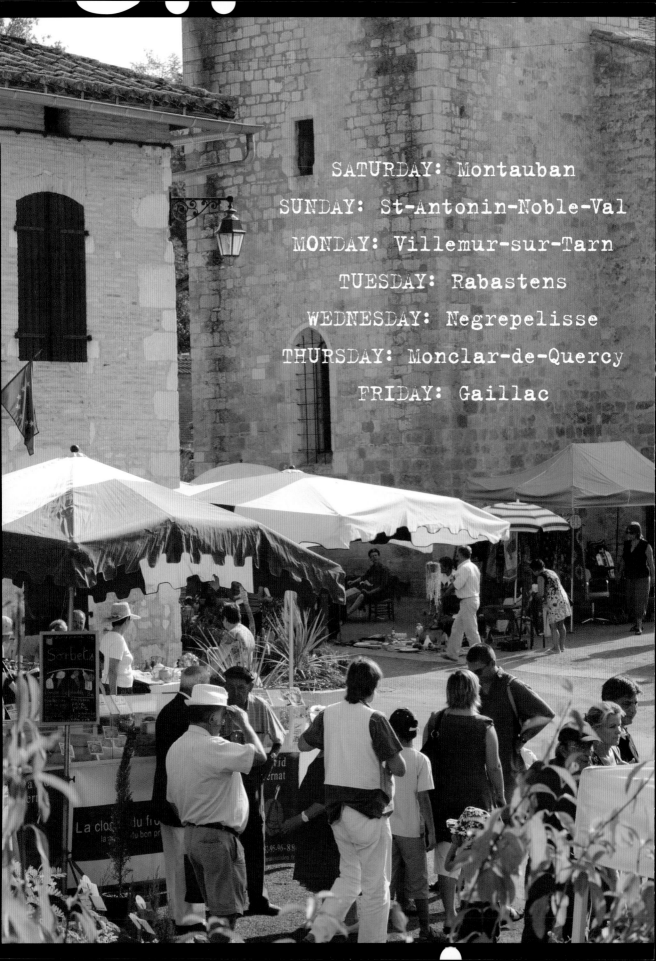

SATURDAY: Montauban
SUNDAY: St-Antonin-Noble-Val
MONDAY: Villemur-sur-Tarn
TUESDAY: Rabastens
WEDNESDAY: Negrepelisse
THURSDAY: Monclar-de-Quercy
FRIDAY: Gaillac

These medieval towns host open-air produce markets every week.

The beefsteak tomatoes, raspberries, *fraise de bois* (small wild strawberries), peaches, farm-raised chicken, fresh eggs, plums, and local Quercy *fromage de chèvre* are all so mouthwatering, it's hard to get home with all purchases intact. Being here for the summer months just makes you want to grow your own fruit and vegetables, raise chickens and cook constantly. That is just what we do.

The Saturday market at Montauban is mind-blowing, set in an avenue of plane trees by the side of the river, the trees Napoleon planted to protect his soldiers from the sun when marching. Hundreds of local farmers bring their food to sell. The integration of French and North African food merchants is now very prevalent. The mixture of exotic spices and the local produce is a recipe for success.

A local *marche aux puces* (flea market), in Vieux, a 1,000-year-old wine village on the banks of the Tarn. One year, my friend the actor John Standing bought an alpine horn from this market as a houseguest gift. The distinctive bellow of the horn has since become an indispensable technique for announcing lunch and calling the troops to the table.

Montauban is home to Ingres, one of France's most important neoclassical painters. It is the oldest of the bastides of southwest France, dating back to 1144. During the 13th century, Montauban suffered from the Inquisition and the Albigensian Crusade to eliminate the Cathars. It was ceded to the English for part of the 14th century and was the headquarters of the Huguenot rebellion in the 17th century, successfully withstanding a siege from Louis XIII. Even today the city embraces Protestantism—rare, as the majority of France is Catholic.

The Midi-Pyrénées is the name of this area that connects the north to the south, the east to the west and is the gate to Spain and on through the Alpes-Maritimes to Italy. It's not where the chic Parisians, informed Americans or backpacking British go. It was off the beaten track when I arrived twenty years ago. Now, with the TGV and improved motorways, it is becoming the new Provence.

The 14th-century Pont Vieux, a remarkable bridge made from Toulousian red brick, still stands, connecting the two sides of town. The Ingres Museum sits on the site of the Counts of Toulouse's castle. This building houses the largest collection of Ingres's work in the world.

Whether in Montauban or my nearest town, Monclar, roaming the labyrinth of narrow streets is the best way to feel a part of the community.

Saturday's market in Montauban is one of the rare times I venture off the farm. It's been the family tradition all these years to go and buy local produce from an array of 300 vendors. It's overwhelming but a feast for the eye, and the reward for maneuvering through the crowds is a *gallupin* (a baby glass of beer) at Café Europe.

The Place Nationale in the center of town is a remarkable square, also made of Toulousian red brick. The arcades are reminiscent of Place des Vosges in Paris. The town comes to life in July, when one of France's major music festivals takes place there.

From Montauban going east towards my nearest small town, Monclar-de-Quercy, is a bundle of exquisite hilltop towns: Bruniquel (which has two chateaux built side by side, cut into the rock of the mountain, where two feuding families lived side by side for many years), Puycelci and Castelnau-de-Montmiral. To the far east of these bastides is Cordes-sur-Ciel. The town was rebuilt after the Albigensian Crusade. Its extraordinary 13th- and 14th-century Gothic architecture has been preserved and reminds me of being in Venice. When French author Albert Camus visited in the 1950s, he famously remarked,

"In Cordes, everything is beautiful, even regret."

What to Buy at the Market

- Tomatoes—all colors and sizes, the largest ones to make sauce.
- Salads—roquette, mâche, mixed greens, butter lettuce
- New potatoes
- Swiss chard
- Radishes (the French eat before meals for their digestion and to stay thin)
- Herbs—large bunches of basil, parsley, mint, thyme (even though we grow them, as they are used daily)
- French beans (some of the growers sell them topped and tailed which is so convenient!)
- Onions—sweet, red, large, small, shallots and garlic (lots of it). Lautrec, not far from us, is the garlic center of France. There is a wonderful garlic festival every August.
- Strawberries, raspberries, blackberries (anything for making jams and Eton Mess)
- Peaches, by the plate
- Goat cheese
- Snails (occasionally)
- Homemade apple juice
- Roasted chickens (to eat for lunch that day)

For many years I couldn't understand what all the fuss was about. Cordes had a perfectly fine square with a café, a car park, the token patisserie and a newsagent. I just hadn't bothered to climb the hill to see what was at the top: a town with views over the Tarn Valley that are truly unforgettable. Touristy but fun, with a yearly medieval carnival, shops that sell Laguiole knives, and a chocolate and sugar museum that enticed the children to put up with the 45-minute drive from "La Castellane," my farm.

I think the first time I discovered all that was waiting at the top of the hill was the week before my fortieth birthday—not long ago! I came across a charming small shop that sold bespoke organic wines. I whizzed in and was attended to by an attractive twenty-something man who was passionate about what he was selling. I left laden with local jams, chocolate-covered raisins, Poire Williams that he distills and case loads of champagne for my birthday. Putting on my best American accent, I asked Laurent Cazzotte if he delivered. I was the first sale of his new store and, yes, he could deliver.

Gaillac is the center of this wine-growing region and home to the Chateau du Fauchard, with amazing gardens by La Notre built for one of Louis XIV's mistresses. Gaillac's wines have been exported to England via Bordeaux since the 10th century.

If you are late to collect the bread.

The baker in Monclar had once been a literature professor at Toulouse University. The bread is custom baked and out of this world and the bakery remains authentic, even to the "trust box" he leaves for you to pay for the bread if he has gone for the day.

the baker leaves the loaves behind the shutters for PICK UP.

FOUACE

2.
The House I Call
La Castellane

I first saw La Castellane late one Sunday morning. It was situated at the end of a long driveway, and all I could say was, "Oh, my God!" I immediately fell in love with it. The simple farmhouse and surrounding buildings reminded me of the fishermen's cottages in Scotland, where my siblings Allister, Mary Jane and Robert and I spent our holidays. The square shape of the house and proportions of the rooms felt almost Georgian, not unlike Dunkathel, Mary Jane's home outside of Cork, Ireland.

Perched on a hilltop, the farmhouse boasted uninterrupted, sweeping views in every direction—fields rolling down to the Tescou River, vineyard land that flattened out and stretched toward the village, and the distant Pyrénées Mountains on the horizon. Wherever you are at La Castellane, the landscapes are breathtaking, even in the dead of winter.

Monsieur and Madame Blaquière, the owners, had lived in the house with various relatives, including her grandparents. Madame Blaquière's ancestors had worked the farmland in the mid-19th century and had lived in the 18th-century pigeonnier before they built the farmhouse as their primary residence. So, by Madame Blaquière's grandparents' standards, the house was quite modern. Mid-20th-century linoleum covered the old

An aerial shot of the house shows the original vineyards, paddocks and grazing fields for the Blonde d'Aquitaine cattle. The old tractor barn is now the dining hall, the room I think of as the heart of the house.

limestone floors, Formica lined the kitchen countertops, and a toilet was boxed off in the large downstairs hallway. The house was by no means in perfect condition, but its welcoming attributes dovetailed neatly with my love for the nonchalant comforts of the European countryside lifestyle.

La Castellane was easier to buy than a pair of shoes. I was so smitten with the house and grounds that I hadn't even noticed that we were surrounded by vineyards. When Monsieur Blaquière uncorked a bottle of rustic peppery red wine, toasted Gary and me as the new owners, and announced that we were inheriting 999 other bottles, I suddenly realized we had just bought a working vineyard.

A snapshot collage of our new French neighbors, who couldn't have been more hospitable and helpful during the protracted renovation period.

I was soon turning what had been a modest 19th-century French farmhouse into the functional equivalent of a small hotel that would soon accommodate all of our friends and family. Finding a local architect to draw a set of accurate floor plans was an expense worth every centime. Of course, the restoration work would not be cheap, but there was nothing in the West Country of England or even the American Midwest that you could buy at this price for fifty acres and a compound of buildings.

I threw myself full swing into renovation, starting with important infrastructure work, like plumbing, roofing, and an electrical system upgrade. Luckily, I was my own client, so I learned from my own mistakes and on my own dime. I ripped the linoleum off the 19th-century floors in every room, rehabilitated the uncovered limestone, and restored the fireplaces throughout the farmhouse. For the first three years, I used the Blaquières' original kitchen until I was able to convert that space into a ground-floor guest room and set up my own kitchen in the cow barn.

The morning sun hits my bedroom and office, where, when alone (which is not often), I enjoy breakfast. The position of the house allows us to enjoy the sun all day long.

Once the basics were installed and the farmhouse became operational, I was able to shift my focus to new renovation challenges. Each year I took on a new project—converting the Pigeonnier into a guesthouse, restoring the *poulailler* into staff accommodations, turning the attics into dormitories for the horde of kids that descend on us every summer and, finally, putting in a swimming pool. This task proved to be the most daunting. For one thing, few swimming pools had been built in the area, so it was hard to find a good local crew to construct it. Once I found the workers, however, it proved to be even harder to keep them on the job and off the Pernod. In addition, they openly sneered at my directions, which seemed to confirm my worst fears about the way French men regard women: as being good only for wearing sexy underwear and eating chocolates. Every time I left the pool site, something would invariably go wrong, so I was forced to stay right there all day every day in the scorching midday sun. I ended up in the Montauban hospital emergency room being treated for dehydration.

Fresh herbs are essential to French cuisine, and nothing is more convenient than an herb garden at arm's reach from the kitchen. I repurposed old wine barrels and stuffed them with aromatic herbs— tarragon, trailing thyme, chervil, summer savory, mint, sweet basil— which we use by the handsful during the hot summer months.

From June on
I run a small
hotel. The only
difference is
no one
gets a bill.

lots of love to you all.
Jennie.

My goal was to create an environment with an unpretentious air, with intimate areas both outside and inside and places where crowds of people could come together to enjoy each other's company without feeling on top of each other. I love the informality of a working farmhouse and that the kitchen is always the center of activity and that the house is in constant use. Though the farm would cease to exist as an ongoing enterprise, La Castellane would become my lab, a place to design my fabrics, to be inspired and, above all, to entertain.

This was the first house I had ever bought, so everything from the acquisition to the renovation involved a huge learning curve for me. Growing up, I had watched my mother working with construction crews, seamstresses, and upholsterers, etc. But now I was the one grappling to pick up the language of building and interior design. It was a baptism by fire.

Wrought-iron daybeds situated under large shuttered windows are perfect lazy-day destinations for a short nap, a sunbath, or just to enjoy a little solitude.

No matter what the time of day, eating and drinking is always a given.

The fifty acres of La Castellane encompasses the hilltop fields where the horses graze all the way to the eucalyptus trees along the banks of the Tescou River at the bottom of the property. On particularly balmy days, we caravan the horses, mini-tractor and hordes of kids down to the riverside for luxuriantly languid picnics that last for hours. I hope these wonderful memories are as **vivid** in the minds of our friends as they are in mine.

3.

Settling In

Although landscaping the grounds around the farmhouse

would take time, we were able to enjoy our vista-vision view immediately by simply throwing down an old picnic rug and buying a paddling pool from the local supermarket and a few deck chairs from Habitat. Voila! Instant room!

It was easy to source armoires, ropey chairs, and chests of drawers from the local flea markets and antiques dealers, but after a thorough cost/benefit analysis, I decided to ship good king-sized mattresses and a hotel's worth of bed linens and towels from the States. Even with shipping costs, importing essential bedroom and bathroom fixtures and furnishings from America is far cheaper than the Euro counterparts. I even crammed all manner of kitchen utensils and accessories into my Audi (being shipped with the beds) that first summer. Apart from being less expensive, I didn't have to run around the entire department of Tarn-et-Garonne with a one-year-old on my hip looking for spatulas and eggbeaters.

From day one, I felt right at home.

Well, make that day two. Due to the frequent and palpable tensions that are known to arise between English ex-pats and French locals, I was slightly anxious about whether or not we would be welcome. But those fears were assuaged when all of the farmers in our area

I had just returned from picking sunflowers in the field when my girlfriend Claudia Rosencrantz snapped this photo. Somehow every moment at La Castellane, even one as banal as collecting my scattered thoughts in the driveway, feels like I'm on the set of a Louis Malle film.

dropped by to greet us with baskets full of homegrown produce. They were thrilled that *les Americans* had moved in. Since then, the Belovoine, Boussenhac, and Escalette families have made our life in France a wonderful experience filled with warmth and joy. My closest neighbor, Elyse Escalette, resides at the farm next door. A remarkable lady, Elyse single-handedly raised her six children. Every morning and evening, she milks her cows, a ritual my children never missed when they were small. Another ritual is her summer lunch party for my entire household. The first year I declined the invitation, protesting that I had far too many houseguests. Her reply was, "I don't mind if there are twenty-five of you!" And all I could say was, "Elyse, we are twenty-seven!" I'll never forget that Sunday lunch. She served seven courses of delicious homemade food with ingredients fresh from her garden. We started off with *saucisson* and ended with her specialty, frozen chocolate mousse. Heaven!

There was a time in the early days of La Castellane when August was filled with people I hardly knew calling out of the blue to say they were en route to Italy, Spain or Portugal and did I know a place in the area where they could stay ...hint hint.

The entry hall today is a far cry
from its previous incarnation.
The haberdasher's table is now
in my London showroom and has
been replaced by a 19th-century
carpenter's workbench.

MOM

Straning MoM

Dogs Barking, car in Driveway,
Purrume, Doorbell.
I remember when you took me out to
dinner on my birthday.
When I'm older can I take you out
to dinner?
I appriciate you making me happy.
Some times when your away I like to think
about you.
I hope you live a long time.
When I'm older I'll still love you.

The boys' art leading up to the attic gives a good indication as to where you are going. Framing is key to making the art look like you are not entering a kindergarten!

Best Houseguests

- Contribute their personalities to the festivities and participate in making the day happen.
- Help out without being asked. Tip the staff well.
- Give presents for the house—things that are needed or stuff for my bath.
- Leave behind sunscreens.
- Groom and tack up horses, clean horse tack.
- Offer to mow the lawn, clean the swimming pool, weed the kitchen garden.
- Buy wine, lots—red, white and rosé.
- Give KI any piece of clothing that she comments on!
- Rent their own car.

Bad Houseguests

- Appear only at meals.
- Expect me to do travel reservations; everyone must have enough French to order a taxi.
- Ask to use my laptop.
- Hog the hammocks.
- Plunk themselves down in the best seats at the table at every meal.

Tips on House Gifts

- Wine
- Chickens, live and attractive, for the chicken coop
- Rose plants
- iPod playlist
- Cookbooks
- Pay for pizza truck on my birthday
- Year of blacksmith fees
- Bunch of handpicked flowers
- Anything for the kitchen
- No fabric items unless vintage or a dress that fits me up top!

A hallway drop spot can be made aesthetically pleasing with the right art and furnishings. India Jane Birley's portrait of one of her father's dogs is a treasured belonging.

4.
The Cow Barn

Although La Castellane never became a year-round residence, it was much more than a holiday home. When the boys were very young and I was still renovating into autumn, they attended the village school up the road. They made friends with the local kids and played soccer in French!

My original plan for the house was to have a formal living room, which was how the cow barn renovation started off; but when I realized that everyone just wanted to be in whatever room I was in—mostly the kitchen—it seemed obvious to set up the kitchen in the larger barn space and abandon any pretense of formality.

Since La Castellane was a second home, it was easier to flout my conventional notions about traditional living spaces. I wanted our French digs to be about fun and easy living, not a place to showcase material finery. "Nothing too precious" became my new motto. The glasses are jam jars, the mismatched plates are cheap flea market finds. If something gets broken, it's *c'est la vie*. The smallest endeavor became a labor of love, and by rolling up my sleeves and getting my

The room now, with the Lloyd Loom dining chairs and the Aga, is as near perfect a room as I could ever want. I wish I could literally pack it up and take it wherever I go.

hands dirty with every aspect of the property—from planting the grounds and maintaining vineyards outside to rehabilitating old floors, adobe walls, and ceiling beams within—I've gained invaluable knowledge that still serves me well, all these many years later, whenever I embark on the sympathetic restoration of an older property.

For years there was always another room to renovate, but the most daunting challenge I ever faced at La Castellane was the task of converting the old cow barn, which attached to the house, into a great room—20th-century nomenclature that denotes a room large enough for eating and living. The cow barn, approximately 40 by 20 feet, had adobe walls and fabulous exposed ceiling beams, imbuing the space with the kind of rural and rustic authenticity that's impossible to fake. I replaced the door to the stable with large French doors that now feel like they open into the scenery itself—expansive countryside of unspoiled farmland, rivers, and forests.

The original farm table that came with the house occupies the kitchen end of the room. On the opposite end, the living area, I angled large, deep English sofas (purchased with money left by a relative for about the price of a secondhand car) around the fireplace. At every time of day, one can find a body or two sunk into the sofa cushions. I converted the old manger into a low shelf for cookbooks, DVDs, and an array of straw shopping baskets.

Although the bones of the room have remained the same since my bovine predecessors, my compulsion to rearrange furniture and replace worn fabric throws the look and layout of the room into a state of constant flux, year after year.

Making it a habit to routinely troll the local flea markets, antique shops, and brocantes for

fabulous vintage furnishings and antiques trains the eye to look beyond an item's first impression and to visualize perhaps veiled possibilities. I so often see something on the second or third trip that didn't jump out at me on the first go-round. These are the pieces that I ultimately fall madly in love with.

A house is not a home if it's all good taste.

You need nutty memorabilia, glaring imperfection, tacky souvenirs! Don't be embarrassed by your life's collection. My kids' artwork is strewn all over my homes. As with everything, actually, presentation is key. Hang non sequitur items in prominent locations. At La Castellane, I move an antique bread paddle from room to room as a portable sculpture and prop it up in various corners when the mood strikes. An ancient heavy iron ring of blacksmith nails I found in the paddock is now looped over a doorknob and serves as an impromptu doorbell.

La Cave (the wine cellar) is a hub, as it services the Dutch barn—which is where most of our meals take place—both before and after meals. The kids and adults congregate to help with preparations and clean up. It's here that all the less attractive pieces of equipment live—freezers, commercial fridges, ice cream and pasta makers, all the tools for being able to cater for so many people. Food is a priority in my life. I don't believe in serving either inferior produce or undrinkable wine. Working hard for the rest of the year enables me to have a cook for these months. Gloria, my fabulous housekeeper for many years, who along with a family member could effortlessly keep house, prepared meals and never ever lost her sense of humour. A key to the success of the summer is who is in the kitchen.

Andrew St. Clair, a childhood friend who comes every summer from Barcelona, is excellent at stirring jam. Tilly LaPaglia, my youngest goddaughter, is my favorite helper in the kitchen.

The Office

When the realtor ushered me into the entrance hall at La
Castellane, the first room I "met" was the Blaquières' salon,
which was off to the right. On the left was the original
kitchen, which I eventually converted into a guest bedroom.
(It's extremely useful to have a bedroom on the ground floor,
especially for elderly family members.) And since I was
constructing a great room in the cow barn, the original
salon became my office. Other than furnishings, the room
required less of an overhaul than the rest of the farmhouse.
I retained the original stone floors and the fireplace with
wood surround. The simple gilt mirror over the mantle was
purchased in Gaillac along with vintage maps of the area,
which shared wall space with my fabric swatches.

GRAND CRU
CLASSE

CHATEAU
IRELAND

Mis En Bouteilles au Chateau
APPELLATION FRONTON

A few years ago I added custom built-in bookshelves for my decorating and art books. Apart from the kitchen counter, it's the only built-in carpentry in the house. I would always rather buy a mobile piece than construct something permanent. After the bookshelves and cabinetry were installed, I splurged on an old Robert Kime sofa and a wonderful tile coffee table by Jacques Adnet.

Before the arrival of Wi-Fi in the area, the office was my private sanctuary; but the other walls in the house are too thick for the signals to go through, so this room has recently become extremely popular with my boys, who need to go online and connect with friends in L.A. When I do find it vacant, the room is still a great place to unwind and relax.

An early incarnation of the office. I picked up the rattan pouf on one of my many trips to Habitat in Toulouse. Since all of the other rooms at La Castellane have doors leading to other rooms or outside, the office was the one room where I could close one door and not be disturbed. Even though I take off months from my L.A. year to be here, I still have to work.

With my life back in Santa Monica, where I am juggling, children, clients, showroom, friends and work force, this place is my refuge, where my most pressing decision is what we are having for lunch! It's how I've survived the madness and fast pace of my other world. It's the reason I have my sanity and am able to work 24/6 from September to early June.

One of my great summer pleasures, along with riding horses, is antiquing. I always bear in my mind a piece of advice from my mother: objects need to either be useful or bring you joy. This principle guides me in my excursions to local flea markets, antiques stores, and village *brocantes* that clutter this unique region of France. A painting, a piece of old china, fun junk jewelry, first-edition Balzac, an amateur woodcut, a silver gelatin photograph, old couture hiding on a dress rack, and an 18th-century frame—these are a few things I've bought and scattered about La Castellane where they blend in and seem completely at home.

The upstairs hallway doesn't just serve as a thoroughfare for the second-floor suite of rooms. I've put it to use as a sitting room—a nice cool and quiet place to escape to when the larger rooms are overcrowded.

The Owl Room

The old hayloft was a large space above the kitchen that housed an owl. Its extra-high ceiling went up approximately two floors. Over the years I had fantasized and daydreamed about what I could do with this remarkable space. My ideas ranged from turning it into my own private apartment, with a bedroom and bath at one end and living room at the other, to designing the room as a great professional workspace, far from the action, where I could really spread out and focus. Now that the boys had commandeered my downstairs office with their laptops, the workplace option seemed like the responsible choice, especially since more and more of my work was taking me to Europe and I desperately needed a place to decamp. But I had also been longing for a tranquil retreat.

Before I knew it, the space I was calling the Owl Room was becoming a Swiss Army knife in a hayloft: extra living room, work space, yoga studio, and screening room. It's mine...and everyone else's. The Owl Room is the perfect place to watch a movie after dinner, and with all the windows flung open, it's like being in an outdoor cinema.

By the time I got around to decorating the Owl Room, both my budget and my taste had expanded to the point where I could skip rummaging through flea markets for good deals and source finer pieces of furniture directly from antiques dealers in the area. For me, the showstopper is the art deco desk, designed by Emile-Jacques Ruhlmann in the 1920s. It, the Charlotte Perriand woven chairs in the foreground and the Danish Mid-Century chair with the lime seat by Niels O.Moller were all purchased in Gaillac from my friend and antiques dealer Antoine de Cadenet. Carpets found in Morocco and the iconic Marilyn silkscreen by Warhol complete the eclectic but strangely harmonious décor.

My desktop is a never-ending,
shape-shifting, mind-bending work
in progress. I usually have five or
six projects going on at once, but
I need chaos to create order.

Even grown-ups need a playroom!

5.
Main House
Bedrooms

That first summer I arrived at the beginning of June with my one-year-old son, Oscar, and spent two weeks getting the house ready for Gary. I wanted my husband's first summer at La Castellane to be the blissful fantasy experience I'd been advertising for months. Unfortunately, Gary's first night at his new French estate was not idyllic.

At 3 a.m. he let out a scream and informed me that he had been bitten—hard. Nonsense, I said; there are no mosquitoes in France. Go back to sleep. But Gary insisted that something had taken a bite out of his hand. I turned on the light to see a very large rat scuttle behind the radiator, its foot-long tail still exposed. I had accidentally left open the door to the hayloft (now the Owl Room) that had provided our rodent intruder access to the house. And Gary had accidentally dangled his arm over the side of the bed in his sleep. So off we went to the hospital in Montauban for a tetanus injection. Needless to say, that drive to the hospital was not the fondest memory of our marriage. All I could do was try to make the case that rat bites in the middle of the night in the French countryside were perfectly normal. At the emergency room, however, the doctor begged to differ.

The task of converting the original kitchen on the first floor into a bedroom turned out to be a piece of gateau. The adjoining pantry could easily become a bathroom. The ceiling was high, a huge luxury in these old farmhouses.

Two of my sons and my beloved Gitana and Greta making themselves comfortable in my room. When the sun comes up, everyone in the world joins me in bed.

Just one of the fabulous aspects of my bedroom is the Juliet balcony. No matter what the season, the doors are always open. In the morning the sun pours in, and at night it's a great and romantic location for stargazing. Old houses generally have great space and rooms with fantastic proportions. My bathroom at La Castellane is the size of most people's bedrooms in L.A. and affords me room for a chair, dressing area, and chest of drawers. I love hanging my clothes on hooks. There's something decorative about displaying colorful clothes, like dresses and nighties, which can almost substitute for art.

Over the years, the fabrics have changed and furniture has been added. For my bedroom I found two somewhat similar armoires and painted them Gustavian Grey. They sit either side of the French doors that lead to the balcony and give the appearance of being a pair—a good trick I learned from a local antiques dealer.

The bedroom across from the Master Bedroom

on the second floor has always been called the Blue Room. The makeshift hanging clothes rack that I rigged up that first summer still remains, even though replacing it with an armoire has been on my "to do" list for over twenty years. When the boys are in residence without friends, they sleep in this room because it's close to me, but when their friends arrive, they migrate up to the dormitory on the third floor and crash out in a mixture of camp, double, and single beds. Since fans have replaced overhead ceiling lighting in all of the bedrooms, I've stationed lamps on bedside tables and dresser tops. Not that I would rely on hideous overhead lighting anyway. There's no substitute for good ambient, situational lighting, even in a kids' room. Good lighting gives texture to their thoughts.

What I didn't know that cold, bleak day in February when I first saw the house was that the bare bushes surrounding the land would explode into a riot of color from the lilacs, roses, and wisteria.

I keep the house full of freshly cut flowers at all times.

An attic room with a sloping ceiling could be a recipe for claustrophobia. But keeping the furniture and fabric to a minimum allows a small room to breathe. Using a small print repeatedly in a small room makes the room seem bigger because your eye isn't ricocheting all over the place. The floral print from my very first collection still holds up all these years later.

That same year, my brothers and I worked on the attic. There were three existing rooms, already divided up, that would clearly serve as the Nursery wing. The boys' room had four beds—one for each of them and one for either Gloria, their nanny, or me. I was trying to wean them from all sleeping with me. Gloria had a room, and then there was one more guest room for visiting nieces and nephews. We turned the hallway into a before-bed movie area. *Les Aristocats* was in heavy rotation that year.

You can never have too many mattresses or duvets to accommodate the overflow.

Keep fabrics simple and color choices to a minimum.

6

The Pigeonnier

The Pigeonnier was the original 18th-century structure at La Castellane. Not only did pigeons courier messages but their dung was used to fertilize the land and was indispensable for a productive vineyard and highly valued in the region. When the price of pigeon dung hit an all-time high in the 19th century, the owners were finally able to build the larger, grander farmhouse and leave the pigeonnier to the birds.

Conventional wisdom holds that all fish and **houseguests** stink after three days. But I have the opposite point of view. Having your **comfort zone** jostled by a few houseguests can actually be quite rewarding. The semi-regular stream of fresh faces that traipse through La Castellane every summer prevents any kind of routine and guarantees the likelihood of surprise or serendipity. The trick is to not think of houseguests as cramping your style. If you can embrace the idea that you can't have loud raucous sex or go to the bathroom with the door open or eat dinner standing over the sink, then you're up for the challenge of taking in a few stragglers.

These charming charcoal drawings by Nigel Waymouth were sketched in the early days when he and his wife, the late Victoria Waymouth, would come and stay. Victoria was one of the great English decorators of our time. The garage was turned into the twin bedroom, and the old bread oven into a bathroom.

It took me a few years to really venture into the building, as it had been partially destroyed by fire in the late 1960s and then allowed to languish into a state of profound disrepair. Any rehabilitation of this structure would be a huge undertaking, but it was the epitome of charm and

I visualized it restored and refurbished, as the ideal guesthouse for La Castellane.

After months of reinforcing infrastructure and extensive remodeling, the Pigeonnier has more than fulfilled its potential and is, in fact, fought over every summer by returning guests.

With the swimming pool built and now more guests than the main house could handle, my brother Robert spent from February to June of 1995 rebuilding and renovating the Pigeonnier.

I have what I call a barracks mentality.

I don't think in terms of individuals; my baseline unit of measurement is the platoon. When I saw La Castellane for the first time, I didn't covet it for my own exclusive pleasure. Without even realizing it, I immediately saw it as a place where my kids could bring their friends, and my friends could bring their kids, and we could all share the unpretentious French country way of living. Fortunately, with the pigeonnier conscripted into service as a guesthouse, the estate can now sleep twenty guests at full capacity. I keep my ten guest rooms as simple as possible because a lot of people want to personalize a room with their own possessions.

To me, the successful guest room is one that functions like a hotel suite—

a clean, neutral space with good mattresses, good pillows and empty closets and dresser drawers. You don't want a guest to find your winter wardrobe stuffed in the closet or extra table linen crammed into drawers. Always have more blankets than you need. I don't mind frayed towels but I can't bear dingy or stained. It's nice to have a couple of good books by the bed and I insist on good reading lamps. Because I spend half my year traveling, I help myself to hotel courtesy soaps and shampoos from all over the world and recycle them in my guest rooms.

My nephew Robin Russell making himself useful. A good guest is someone who helps and mucks in. Age is not important.

The bread paddle in the corner is a decorative
and historic relic from the original property. The
framed photograph is by Marie Laure de Decker,
one of France's most loved photographers.

When a house guest arrives, I won't be sweeping down the staircase in some flowing number on cue. I usually greet people from my bathroom window, shouting to come on in and open a bottle of Bandol. I'm a very easygoing hostess. I only require that guests embrace the communal spirit of the environment. My overall advice to newcomers is very simple: be up for anything. I like doers and guests who are generous with their time. I love it when a guest offers to cook lunch for the group or organizes a game of soccer or boules before dinner.

Guests who are motivated to be hands-on are always invited back. Whether they're tending the kitchen garden or feeding the horses, none of these gestures go amiss. Everyone is free to do whatever inspires them all day, but sharing the big meal at night is de rigueur. It's a time when kids are encouraged to talk and interact with adults. It's all about communication, friendship and eye contact.

The area at the back of the living quarters had been ruined by fire. It is now a fab little kitchen with its own washer—crucial when you have so many guests.

Guest Room Must-Haves

- Comfortable beds and pillows
- Lavender bags on the pillows and in armoires
- Somewhere to hang clothes, even if it's a few pegs
- A table or surface to lay out makeup
- Cut flowers
- Chocolates or fruit from the orchard
- Carafe of water
- Candle by the bed in case the electricity goes out
- Small mat by the bed if the floors are stone or tile
- A list of house rules
- Mosquito deterrent plug ins

Must-Not-Haves

- No old clothes stored in the closets
- No extra blankets for the house crammed into every drawer
- Nothing under the bed
- No stained towels or sheets
- No surfaces with your photographs and other memorabilia
- No sign of the guest who was there before
- No broken things—fans, alarms, lights

Windows now cover the opening where
the pigeons flew in and out. The bed is
from my teenage years in London.

This bedroom was the original kitchen where the farmers lived here in the late 18th century. Due to the fire sometime in the 1960s, the fireplace was badly damaged. So I decided to turn this room into a good-sized guest room. The beauty of this room, and in fact all of the rooms, is that the Quercy stone absorbs the heat and keeps both this and the farmhouse extremely cool. Only overhead fans are necessary on even the hottest days.

Something I learned from the neighboring farmers' wives early on was to open the shutters early in the morning to let in the cool air for about an hour, then keep the shutters closed until dusk. It's amazing how cool the rooms stay.

Having **guest rooms** you don't use is a form of **hoarding.**

The hostess/houseguest relationship is very much like a dance. You're always moving in relation to each other. You're following someone's lead or they're following yours. Most people instinctively know the steps.

Here are a few houseguest tips for anyone who thinks they have two left feet:

- Don't interrupt my afternoon snooze in the hammock under the beech tree with some mundane question about whether Easy Jet flies at night.

- Don't terrify the children or adults with tales that the house is haunted, as one guest did when she asked to be moved because ghosts were scratching their way out of graves underneath her bed. They may well have been, but let's not frighten the others.

- Don't stub your cigarettes out in the potted plants or drop them in the gravel driveway. Woe betide the smoker whose cigarette butt I find and can trace back to them.

- Don't go to the market and buy just enough food for yourself. *Mon dieu!* I don't expect much. A crate of peaches in France is ten Euros. Spring for it. This isn't an episode of *Survivor, France*.

- I don't love walking into a room and finding an unmade bed.

- Don't dump your laundry in the laundry room. The only time that's okay is when you're literally on the way to the airport, at which point I think it's polite for the houseguests to rip the sheets off their beds themselves.

- I'll bend over backwards to share and entertain, but it's a communal effort, so please pitch in.

There's nothing that **fabric and flowers** can't transform.

Off the twin bedroom (previous page) is a lean-to bathroom I tiled with mosaics left over from the pool construction. Newly installed French doors make it accessible from the pool as well.

When the boys were very young and attended school in the village, our adorable little pony Scrappy was their mode of transportation to and from Verlhac. Here is Scrappy at his favorite spot behind the Pigeonnier, escaping the midday sun by the washing line. No one wants washed laundry blowing in their face, but in the French countryside in the summer, it's part of everyday life. Instead of using epic amounts of BTUs, I let nature do the work for me and harnessed the power of the sun and lovely lilac-scented breezes to line-dry my clothes and sheets. Detergent manufacturers have spent millions trying to infuse their products with "fresh" scents. Sorry—no substitute for the real deal.

I dream of being invited to dinner on the Pigeonnier terrace, a great dining area for more intimate meals. Sheaves of dried lavender hang on exterior walls, providing aroma therapy.

7.
The Gardens

The long driveway that winds its way up
to the farmhouse cuts through acres of pastureland. The
idea of an ornamental garden was not appealing to me. A lot
of people want to go to the country and trim hedges and
plant mums, but I wanted to be very un-busy with that kind
of work. Anything that is so time-consuming and that can
fall apart without the proper attention was exactly what I
didn't want in a property that was to be a summertime
residence.

As I planned to use the outdoors as an extension of the
house, creating proper grounds was a top priority. I wanted
the property to look organic and feel faithful to the
natural habitat. All I had to do was reclaim the overgrown
and unkempt pastureland surrounding the house. That meant
tilling the land and turning it over, getting rid of stones,
doing a bit of contouring, and then we just had to start
mowing—year after year. Eventually our efforts were rewarded
with a perfectly serviceable dense carpet of...mown field.

With the French doors constantly open, the house seems to
flow outside from every room and into the grandeur of the
unspoiled French countryside. These ancient landscapes of
vivid colors and textures, devoid of suburban clutter, look
much like they did hundreds of years ago when they inspired
Cezanne, Corot, Monet, and Van Gogh.

After many years of enjoying a kitchen garden behind the
house, an ash seeded itself there and grew to such a height
that the garden was not getting enough sun. The vineyard to
the right of the driveway had to be pulled out due to some
kind of root rot, so suddenly there was a perfect space for a
tennis court—or a good-sized kitchen garden. As much as I
love tennis, my love for food won the day.

The small brick building houses the well, which is still
viable. Stones collected from around the property support
the large stone trough once used for the farm animals.
The water is delivered via the well. The trough is also
handy for rinsing the vegetables from the kitchen garden.

One of the things I most enjoy on the long summer nights is the sound of the combine working over-time. It might irritate some people to hear the harvester in the field late at night until early in the morning, but I find it to be very soothing.

One of the beauties of summer in France is going to Elyse's farm at the foot of our driveway every day at five o'clock to get our milk straight from the cows. It's always a kick with children who live in a city to learn where milk comes from. Drinking fresh milk from cows that I know and see on a daily basis is a rare experience in this day and age.

The excitement of arriving in the spring and prepping the land for planting is something that is either in your blood or not. Watching tomatoes, artichokes, peppers and courgettes grow each day is thrilling to my boys and me. Each morning, sometimes before coffee and breakfast, we dash up to the garden to measure the progress of our vegetables.

The "starter hens" that we bought with Ben Goldsmith at market are now twenty. We let them out into the outdoor living room of their *poulailler* in the morning and lock them up in the evenings so as to avoid any predators.

From early June to late August, the ripening fruits from the fig, cherry, plum, and apple trees determine what jams we eat, what marinades are made and, most importantly, what desserts are created. This is heaven to me. My mind so easily transitions from one set of problems to another. But these are good problems. What to cook for dinner— how can that be a problem?

8.
Everyone to the Table

From the moment we wake up in the morning to the aroma of fresh croissants warming in the Aga to filling the dishwasher late at night, food and eating are an integral part of life at La Castellane.

The key is to make meal preparation as easy and as fun as possible. Otherwise, who wants to be in the kitchen on a sweltering summer day when everyone else is out by the pool? Guests that cook are very popular with me.

One time I forgot I had invited guests for a barbecue and decided to go for a horseback ride. On my return, I found some rather irate guests who were apparently expecting dinner before midnight!

Perfection is not a word I use when decorating or entertaining. Mixing up everything from the dinnerware to the candles to the guests is what makes for a successful evening. At my table, old-fashioned etiquette goes slightly to the wind. You can move around during dinner. You can start or finish when you like. If everyone had to wait for the hostess to sit down before they ate, they'd go hungry.

But "please" and "thank you" never go out of style.

Candlelight and adobe walls are the PERFECT backdrop for an unpretentious meal.

Ratatouille

- 4 tablespoons olive oil
- 4 cloves garlic, crushed and minced
- 2 large onions, quartered and thinly sliced
- 2 small aubergines, cubed
- 4 green bell peppers, coarsely chopped
- 8 large tomatoes, coarsely chopped, or 2 cans (14.5 ounces each) diced tomatoes
- 6 small zucchini, cut into 1/4-inch slices
- 2 teaspoons dried basil leaf
- 1 teaspoon dried oregano leaf
- 1/2 teaspoon dried thyme leaf
- 4 tablespoons chopped fresh parsley

Preparation: In a 4-quart Dutch oven or saucepan, heat olive oil over medium heat. Add garlic and onions and cook, stirring often, until softened, about 6 to 7 minutes. Add eggplants; stir until coated with oil. Add peppers; stir to combine. Cover and cook for 10 minutes, stirring occasionally to keep vegetables from sticking.

Add tomatoes, zucchini, and herbs; mix well. Cover and cook over low heat about 15 minutes, or until eggplant is tender but not too soft.

Warm Potato Salad

This is great alongside barbecued meats and vegetable. Boil a pound of new potatoes until just cooked through. Meanwhile, whisk together 1/2 cup of crème frâiche with 3 tablespoons of grainy mustard and a dollop of soft butter in a large mixing bowl. Once the potatoes are cooked through, strain them and add them to the sauce. Serve immediately with sliced chives sprinkled on top.

Informality is all about a lack of fuss and bother and an excess of simplicity. Food, friends and a view—you're done. Oh, and of course, wine.

Salad Niçoise à la Castellane

This salad is an entire meal and I like to give it to unsuspecting newcomers as an opening lunch or dinner. Although it's not a typical addition, I like to include melon since we have melon farms all around us, and often when there is a glut the farmers cannot give them away. Serve with warm breads from the organic baker in Montclar. You need to order the bread in advance; pickup is after noon, or he will leave it for you inside the closed window shutter if he is having lunch. It's hard to arrive home with the loaf, as it's warm and can so easily be torn apart. If you miss him and haven't put in your order, go to the 8 a Huit at the roundabout. By the way, 8 a Huit does not mean what it says. It's open from 9 to 7; in the summer it can stay open later, but you have to check. The French have their own rules!

Serves 16-20

- 2 pounds fresh tuna steaks (best from fishmonger on rue de la Résistance in Montauban)
- extra virgin olive oil
- coarse salt and freshly ground black pepper
- 1-1/2 pounds cherry tomatoes, halved
- 1 pound haricots verts, topped and toed, steamed and cooled
- 1 pound new potatoes, scrubbed, steamed and cooled
- 6 eggs (best collected from the chicken coop), hardboiled and peeled, cut in half
- 2 small cantaloupes, peeled, seeded and sliced (locally grown are arguably the best in the world)

Rub the tuna with olive oil and generously season with salt and pepper. Grill over a hot fire or pan fry it just until the outside is cooked but the inside is still pink. There's nothing worse than anything overcooked. Break up the tuna and arrange alongside the haricots verts, potatoes, eggs and melon. Serve with Best Vinaigrette if you'd like.

Barbecuing My Way

I barbecue often and grill a lot of different foods at once. Leftovers will always be polished off late at night or for breakfast the following day with eggs. I marinate chops, Toulousian sausage, chicken pieces and steaks. Usually the marinade is made from preserves that were put up the year before... something figgy, tomatoe-y, or anything we had in abundance. For example, fig chutney whisked with a bit of olive oil and vinegar is terrific with chicken. Cherry preserves thinned with olive oil and slathered on pork is lovely. I let the meats marinate for a few hours. The most important step of barbecuing is to find the most competent grill-master in your group and urge them to take on the job. Vine cuttings from last year's pruning of the vineyard is the best fuel source, and that's what we use for all of our barbies. Once the fire is hot and ready and the meat is on, I like to slice aubergines, red peppers, tomatoes, onions, and leeks and marinate them in olive oil and just a splash of balsamic vinegar and place them alongside the sizzling meats. Nothing is more delicious than crispy aubergine.

Best Vinaigrette

Gently sauté two very crushed cloves of garlic in 1/4 cup olive oil until the oil is fragrant, about 2 minutes. Let the oil cool, then mash the garlic cloves with the back of a fork. Whisk the oil and garlic together with a tablespoon of balsamic vinegar, a teaspoon of grainy mustard, and the merest sprinkle of sugar. Mix all ingredients together, just to combine them, but not so much that it becomes too thick.

Soufflé for two is never on the agenda at La Castellane, but cut roses always are. Jam jars should never be thrown away! They have many uses as containers for flowers, candles and new jams.

Courgette Quiche

There is always a surplus of *courgettes* (zucchini) in the garden at summer's end, and a quiche is the perfect place to use them. Slice 4 *courgettes* thinly and sauté them in a bit of olive oil until slightly soft, if you have the time. You can leave them raw. Any which way, lay a rolled-out pastry crust in a tart shell and pour in 6 eggs that you've whisked together with a dollop of soft butter, salt and pepper, and a tablespoon of crème fraîche. Spread the sliced *courgettes* evenly over the egg mixture. If you'd like, sprinkle the quiche with grated cheese. I like Brebis, a hard goat cheese from the Pyrénées. Bake the quiche in a 375-degree oven until set and lightly browned, about 30 minutes.

Rustic Onion Tart

CRUST: Work together 6 tablespoons of cold unsalted butter, 1 rounded tablespoon lard (or vegetable shortening), 1 heaping teaspoon baking powder, 1/2 teaspoon salt and two cups sifted flour with your hands or a pastry blender until the mixture resembles coarse meal. Add enough cold milk (about 4 tablespoons) to make a firm dough. One beaten yolk can be added if desired. Line a pie plate with rolled pastry or press the dough into the ridged sides of a 12-inch tart pan with removable bottom.

FILLING: Cook 3 slices of bacon in a large skillet until crisp, then transfer to paper towels to drain. Grate 3 large onions in a food processor. Add 2 tablespoons butter to a skillet. Fry grated onions until much reduced and nicely browned. Add 1 tablespoon flour and stir well. Add 1 teaspoon salt, 1 teaspoon black pepper, and 1/2 teaspoon freshly grated nutmeg. Beat three large eggs until light and mix with 1 cup of heavy crème fraîche. Fold this into the fried onions gently until mixed. Pour into crust and bake at 400 degrees for 30 minutes, or until brown and puffy. Serve hot or at room temperature.

Tomato and Courgette Pizza

The genius thing about the French supermarket is the roll-out,
pre-prepared pastry. Brise, Sable, Feuillette, etc. This is how
I survived in the early years when it was me rushing to do
pick-ups from the airport, changing sheets, making dinner; it
was only when the beloved Dr. Cornelius put me into the
hospital with exhaustion that I realized I needed to delegate.
Anyhow, the pastry, of such excellent quality, can be used for
pizza, quiche, tarte tatin, any kind of vegetable; it all
really depends on what's ready in the garden. This pizza is
one of my favorites, especially since there is always a
plethora of *courgettes* (zucchini), which often, before you know
it, grow to church fête size.

- 1 portion of packaged pastry dough
- flour for rolling
- 2 cups Homemade Tomato Sauce
- 4 small courgettes, thinly sliced
- coarse salt
- freshly ground black pepper

Preheat oven to 400 degrees F or 200 degrees C.

Dust your work surface with flour and roll out the tart. Place
the thinly rolled tart on a cookie sheet and bake blind for
5 minutes. Remove from the oven and evenly spread with the
tomato sauce. Layer the *courgettes* (of course, you can add on
other vegetables as well, but I can't bear to hear "What's
that?" so I tend to keep it simple). Sprinkle the entire pizza
with salt and pepper and bake for about 15-20 minutes, or until
the *courgettes* are cooked through and lightly browned. Serve
immediately. I make at least two of these and sometimes three,
depending on how many we are.

Gazpacho

This is the recipe that Otis and I like to make together. It's simple and easy and requires no cooking!

Serves 12-16

- 9 pounds overripe tomatoes, blanched and peeled
- 6 red bell peppers, seeded and roughly chopped
- 6 small cloves garlic, peeled and roughly chopped
- 3 large cucumbers, peeled, seeded and roughly chopped
- 1 cup olive oil
- 1/2 cup red wine vinegar or sherry vinegar
- coarse salt
- freshly ground black pepper
- Tabasco or your favorite hot sauce
- 21 large basil leaves

Using a blender or food processor, puree the tomatoes, peppers, garlic, cucumber, olive oil and vinegar together. When mixed to your liking (I like it to be a bit lumpy, not too much) season to taste with salt, pepper and hot sauce. Put the gazpacho into a container and refrigerate for a few hours; or if done at the last minute, add large pieces of ice to cool it. Serve with torn up basil and another dash of Tabasco. Serve with warm bread.

Intimate dining spots are set up around the property for when the guest count is low. The early evening soccer games are played in this area; everyone joins in, either as spectator of participant.

Apricot tart, a bottle of homemade raspberry cordial, and flowers from the field are set off when placed on coordinating but unmatched fabrics.

Homemade Tomato Sauce

From mid-July until the end of summer there is a surplus of tomatoes in the kitchen garden. I can't bear waste, so a great activity for houseguests is to see who can make the best tomato sauce. This simple one is my favorite.

Yields about 2 cups

- 3 pounds ripe tomatoes
- extra virgin olive oil
- 1 small yellow onion, finely diced
- 1 clove garlic, crushed
- coarse salt
- freshly ground black pepper
- 1 teaspoon or so sugar
- small handful fresh basil leaves

Blanch the tomatoes; peel them and discard the skins. Dice them, being sure to reserve all their lovely juice.

Heat a few spoonfuls of olive oil in a heavy saucepan over medium-high heat. Add the onion and sauté until softened but not browned, about 5 minutes. Add the tomatoes and bring to a boil and let it bubble for about 5 minutes. Add the garlic and a large pinch each of salt and pepper, and turn the heat to low. Let the sauce simmer for 45 minutes. Stir in the sugar to taste at the last minute. (There's something in the chemistry between tomatoes and sugar that you need to get just right, and the amount depends on the acidity of the tomatoes. Just taste it.) Finish the sauce by tearing in the basil leaves.

Melon and Parma Ham

This is completely irresistible for breakfast, lunch or dinner. At 1 euro a melon, it's both a steal and a taste that only the gods should know about. It's sweet, it's savory and is perfection when made with slices of the thinnest cut ham from anywhere in Spain. Now, that's a great house present! A ham from Spain. My lovely friend Tony Pinas brought me one about 12 years ago from Barcelona and I remember thinking, "what a classy gift." It lasts forever and you can do so much with it. I like gifts that everyone can benefit from.

Roasted Red Pepper Herb Dip

Place 2 whole red peppers directly on a medium-to-high flame on a gas stovetop or grill. (Alternately, brush peppers with oil and place on a sheet pan in a 450-degree oven for 15-20 minutes, or until the skin starts to slightly brown and loosen.) Rotate the peppers using metal tongs until the skin is charred and blackened. Place the peppers in a bowl and cover tightly with plastic wrap. Once cooled, peel off the skin and remove seeds. Place peeled peppers in a food processor along with 3 cloves chopped garlic, 10 leaves chopped basil, 1/4 cup chopped parsley, juice of 1/2 lemon, 8 ounces sour cream, 1 tablespoon Worcestershire sauce, 1 teaspoon paprika (preferably smoked), 1 teaspoon Tabasco, and salt and pepper to taste. Blend until smooth. Refrigerate for 1 hour before serving. Serve with toasted baguette slices and fresh crudités.

Plum Clafouti

Butter a pie plate or baking dish and sprinkle it with a couple tablespoons of sugar. Evenly spread 8 or 9 plums, pitted and halved, over the sugar, skin side down. Use more plums if you need to. In a blender, blend 3/4 cup milk, 3/4 cup light cream, 3/4 cup flour, 2 eggs, 1 egg yolk and 1/4 teaspoon of salt for two minutes. Add 1/4 cup sugar and 1-1/2 teaspoons vanilla. Blend the mixture a few more seconds and pour it over the plums. Bake the clafouti in the middle of a 400-degree oven for about 30 minutes, or until puffed and golden. Lightly dust the clafouti with sugar and serve at once.

Plum Chutney

In a bowl, combine 1-1/2 cups of chopped pitted prunes and 1 cup of water. Cover with plastic wrap and microwave at high for 2 minutes, or until prunes are plumped. (You can also plump the prunes with boiling water.) In a saucepan, heat 2 tablespoons of extra virgin olive oil until shimmering. Saute a chopped small red onion over medium-high heat until softened, about 5 minutes. Add 1 seeded and chopped plum tomato and cook until slightly softened, about 3 minutes. Add 2 teaspoons mustard seeds, 1/2 teaspoon cinnamon, 1/2 teaspoon freshly grated nutmeg and 1/2 teaspoon crushed red pepper, and cook until fragrant, about 1 minute. Stir in the prunes and their liquid, 2-1/2 tablespoons sherry vinegar, 3 tablespoons light brown sugar, and a pinch of salt; simmer over medium-low heat, stirring occasionally, until the mixture becomes jamlike, approximately 25 minutes.

This chutney can be refrigerated for up to two weeks.

Most of the plum trees in this region are used for making prunes. Plums are extremely versatile and wonderful stewed in Cahors wine, as an ingredient in other fruit jams, and my favorite—plum chutney.

Eton Mess

I am not sure where the name came from. Did a bunch of Etonians come up with this dessert? Anyway, it's something that takes 15 minutes to prepare and can be used with raspberries, strawberries, blackberries or a mixture. The boys especially love getting their hands dirty with all of the ingredients.

Serves 16

- 4 pints fresh mixed berries (raspberries, strawberries, blackberries and red currants)
- sugar if needed
- 4 large meringues (there is a lady right opposite Antoine's who makes the best meringues; otherwise get from Leclerc), about 2 cups crushed
- 2 cups whipping cream
- 2 cups crème frâiche

Mash the berries so that they form their own sauce. Add sugar to the mashed berries to taste. Whip the cream until stiff peaks form and fold in the crème frâiche. With clean hands (that are willing to get messy), crush and mix together the meringues, cream mixture and berries. Place in the fridge and serve chilled.

Frozen Syllabub
Yields 2 quarts

I love to make this with *framboise de bois*, which are out of this world; but I usually have to buy them, as when picking them from the garden I eat them, as does everyone. If you can scramble together enough raspberries and strawberries (a quart), wash them, leave them to dry in a colander and get out the crème frâiche and the heavy cream (1 cup each). Puree the berries together in a food processor with the creams. Add a dash of sugar if needed and then put in the freezer. Once frozen, scoop into tall champagne glasses that you buy at every *brocante*.

On-hand Essentials for Impromptu Entertaining

- Foie Gras
- Bottle of Sauterne
- Olives
- Blinis
- Sparkling water
- Variety of juices
- Taramaslata
- Rice
- Hummus
- Goat cheese
- Fresh baguette
- Pasta
- Pesto sauce
- Tomato sauce
- Tea lights
- Laundered napkins

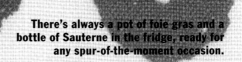

There's always a pot of foie gras and a bottle of Sauterne in the fridge, ready for any spur-of-the-moment occasion.

9.
Outdoor Life

The early years were all about bartering. That was, until I got

my horses. The Bouzanhacs, who live to the east of my property, took care of my land and swapped bales of hay for foie gras. That came to an end with the arrival of my exquisite black Arabs, Nazullah and Osiris. I give my favorite couple, Carrie and Andrew—who I had meet in the Loire valley at a girlfriend's chateau—full credit for the appearance of these mares. I had mentioned that I would love to have some horses to ride, as the countryside is so perfect, with no fences and full of *chemin rurales*. I happened to mention that they had to be very beautiful, as they would be in the paddock going down the driveway, and I didn't want any old nags!

One of the first guests at La Castellane was my friend the actress Fran Drescher. We had met during the shooting of a pilot in San Diego with Gary and Dan Aykroyd. While we were sitting by the pool on location, I invited (as I tend to do) everyone to come stay with me in France. I had been in France for a few days when the phone rang. To my surprise, it was Fran on the line. "Sweetie, how's next week? Have you got room?" she asked. Before I had time to reply, she gave me her flight number.

How I got three boys on a horse in the middle of a sunflower field all looking angelic is a mystery to me now. If I didn't have this photo, I'd never believe it.

Fran loved the view and the house. Her only comment was "Where's the patio furniture?" It had never occurred to me to have anything more than an old blanket to drag out and place under the large oak tree. I have since spent a fortune on outdoor furniture, which is worthwhile, as only the good stuff lasts.

Once the important pieces for outside had been bought, the smaller tables, chairs, benches and umbrellas were found at flea markets. Old wrought-iron beds (the more chipped the paint, the better) make wonderful seating, and mattresses and pillows made from water-resistant outdoor fabric worked perfectly for them. I am now working on my first collection of outdoor fabrics; the patio furniture has given me inspiration. I am always on the lookout for good patio furniture.

The year Tricia Brocke, my best L.A. girlfriend, came to visit, she and her daughter, Cleo, stayed for a few weeks. (While there, she faxed her third husband to inform him that their short marriage was over. As Tricia says, sometimes you have to marry to realize it's over.) I remember the heat being intense. The Tour de France went right past the driveway. And I was to meet the director of my dreams, Louis Malle. He and his wife, Candice Bergen, were sort of "neighbors"; they lived about an hour away. On Tricia's invitation, we went to their house for lunch. And there, under the shady oak tree, was the white plastic supermarket furniture that I so hated, but there it looked so chic. Suddenly, this furniture was all that I wanted, but I would have to wait until the next summer; it was all sold out.

It's all about endorsement!

Essential to French country living are bicycles and horses. I make sure to have a full complement of bicycles to accommodate guests of every age, from three-wheelers to bikes for rugged terrain.

The unequivocal **highlight** of the summer is August 4, a birthday

I share with Barack Obama and the late Queen Mother. The oldest of my hardcore friends are at La Castellane that week, so there's pretty much "no room at the inn" for last-minute drop-ins.

My ex-husband, Gary, started a ritual that has lasted almost twenty years. He surprised me our first summer in residence with a mobile pizza truck that arrived early in the evening to cater my party. All these years later, Pier and his van arrive a few hours before everyone else to set up, enjoy a few aperitifs, and prepare the doughs and toppings for the most sumptuously delicious pizza I've ever had anywhere in the world. All we have to do is organize the bonfire, make sure the guitars are tuned, and fill the old yogurt glass jars with tea lights. The last few years I have been given giant wishing lanterns. To any passerby in the valley below, our hillside must look like the landing site for an alien invasion. In the past we have had various bands and DJs. Budgie

from Souixsie and
the Banshees played
drums one summer. I've
also had a karaoke
birthday and impromptu
variety shows, but
no voice has ever
been as extraordinary
as Sabina, the lead
singer from the
Brazilian Girls.

   I am always last
to appear at any of
my parties, and my birthday night is no exception. As my
bedroom overlooks the driveway, I can greet my guests from
my balcony and coerce them up to help me dress. I love the
twilight hour, when the sun has settled, the heat has calmed
down and it's time to open every color of wine.

Hammocks and swinging ladders tur

To watch one's kids grow and develop with a colorful, lively, rotating cast of friends and family from all over the world was a childhood dream I was able to realize. Everyone knows I'm not an heiress. I work very hard for my money. And when my accountant tells me at the end of every year how much my summer cost me, it's always a shock. But the reason I work so hard is precisely so I can splurge on houseguests for three long, hot months and create wonderful memories for the people I love.

a tree into an amusement park.

the best –!
Thank you again
Lots and Lots
of love

Hermione
xxxx

Katherine –

We have been so happy
here – a wrench to leave.
Kidnapping your eldest to
keep a piece of the family
with us as long as possible!!

Have a great summer/
birthday. See you in Goa –
– Mexico – wherever
Enormous quantities
luvv + thanks.

Gina xx

Essex SS42DZ

15/July 06

Dear Kathryn,
        What a wonderful time I had
with you in France. I had a lovely
holiday thanks to you and Ale.

        What would I do without friends
like you. I was as you know in a
low state after the past 3 months.
and now I'm ready for what
may come.

        Give my regards to Alastair and
your Mother if she is still as keen
we could do with some French
weather in this country right now.

        My foots healing and on
Monday I go into Hospital for
an angiogram for my angina.
Wish me luck!   Yours Max

---

21 CROOKHAM ROAD
LONDON SW6 4EG
TEL: 020 7371 0273

Dear Kathryn,
        I had such an amazing
time in France – thank you
so much for being such an
incredible hostess....
I loved meeting Andrew and
Orlando and all your boys
are so amazing. I really did
have such a fun time and
especially enjoyed sleeping
under the stars. I hope you
have a relaxing rest of the
summer and we meet soon
either in LA, London or even
India – I can't explain how
much fun I had – you are

August 4, 1996

XXXX Always.
C

8-5-96
Gracias por todas las cosas
buenas. el tiempo corre si se
comparte con personas como
Fantasticas como ustedes en
Especial. Kat. Braunx and
the boys los adoro
a todos. Love
Gloria

6th August 1996

(Auckland — France)

August 96

Kath—
Here are your yummy little gummy
bears! They are so gorgeous — I really
miss them — they made being away
from Oliver and Trinity a little easier
Thank you again so much for everything
and hopefully I shall be seeing you some
time in July when I bring the whole
gang over and we will be neighbours!
keep me posted on the house and enjoy
yourself — you are truly in paradise.

Take care,

Dear Otis: At last the
long promised camera. There
is a film already in it &
2 more for later. Adjust
for sun, shade. Here's to
the new Cecil Be
Love Sus

Ithaka — Roddam
FLYNN
Marina Cooper me Casa Su Casa
4th of July 95   merci

wish, that one day I will have a "potager"
thanks a lot.
A Bientot Katherine.

IT WAS REAL

Darling Kathryn,

I've just come back from my annual holiday at La Castellane.
It is pouring with rain in London (of course, it's August)
and I'm already wearing winter clothes. But once again a
week in France with you and your boys and your friends has
restored me. I feel so lucky that we are always included in
your summers in France. It's the most time I spend
uninterrupted with my children all year.

There is a magic about your house, and the magic is all
about you and your unique energy. You have the most open
heart and it is reflected in the atmosphere of the house.
There is such a feeling of welcome, and of acceptance,
everyone can be themselves there, and that is why it is
always such fun. You invite practically everyone you meet,
and somehow it always works.

What I love about staying with you is the sense of
familiarity and the element of the unexpected, as, let's face
it, anything can happen under your roof! Our children have
grown up with each other and have a deeper bond than I think
they are conscious of...just like you and me, who have known
each other since we were six.

I love the early morning rides through the sunflowers, the
long dinners in the barn looking out at the moon, the boys'
banter by the pool, the birthday parties for you with the
pizza truck from the village, the bike rides being chased by
local rottweilers, lying on the bed under the trees looking
at the stars, and most of all your humour. I never laugh as
much anywhere as there with you.

And as my son Lyle put it, as we boarded the plane home at
Toulouse a few days ago, you're a 'real one-off'.

Love you,
Cosi xxx
Lady Cosima Somerset

Resources

Albi

Pre en Bulle
9 Lices Jean Moulin
81000 Albi
After lunch, go to the Toulouse Lautrec Museum. A perfect day is to visit Mme Palmier in her early 18th-century farmhouse on the banks of the Tarn to paint and sculpt in her amazing studio. Then to on to lunch in Albi.

Bruniquel

There are a few places to eat, simple French food, nothing that stands out except for the pizzeria, which is on the way up towards the chateau on the left side of town.

Castelnau de Montmiral

It's the least photogenic of the three towns. In the Place des Arcades, which dates back to the 13th century, there are a couple of restaurants worth eating at: Auberge des Arcades and La Table des Consuls.

Cordes-sur-Ciel

There are antique shops on the way in town that are worth looking into. It doesn't matter which restaurant you go to in main square; they all serve simple food. Chèvre Salad is what I order in any of these places. The cheese is always local and fresh.

Le Tonneau des Saveurs
5 Grand rue de l'Horloge
81170 Cordes-sur-Ciel
On the way to the top, stop off and visit Marina and Laurent Cazotte's jewel of a store. They have a great selection of "biologique" wines. Laurent will arrange for wine tastings, tours of the local vineyards.

Gaillac

Distillerie Artisanale Cazottes
Organic Spirits and Wines
Le Carlus
81130 Villeneuve sur Vere
05 63 56 85 39
The Cazotte family run distillery between Cordes and Gaillac with its original machinery is fun to visit for all ages, and at the same time stock up with wines. Laurent's Poire William is the best there is. Not that I am a connoisseur of liquors, but I gave a bottle to Mark Birley, the legendary founder of Annabel's nightclub from London, and he immediately ordered it for all clubs.

Vigne en Foule
Wine bar and restaurant
80 Place de la Liberation
81600 Gaillac
The best local restaurant in Gaillac. After the Friday produce market this is the place to go.

L'Ancienne Auberge
Puycelci
81140
05 63 33 65 90
If you're wanting to have a proper lunch or dinner, go to L'Ancienne Auberge. Dorothy, the owner/chef, is from the States.

Salvagnac

Romain Gerard
Grand 'rue
81 630 Salvagnac
05 63 33 99 98
06 08 55 54 81 (mobile)
Furniture in metal and wood along with some antiques left (very big mirrors, huge bookcases etc.).

Claude Palmier
Art teacher
jean.palmier@wanadoo.fr

Daniel de la Falaise
Chef
daniel@danieldelafalaise.fr
His approach to cooking celebrates immediacy, raw ingredients and natural methods of production.

Design Bootcamp
www.kathrynireland.com
I host design courses at La Castellane to fast track you to my design philosophy, while taking in the French country and all it has to offer.

Picnics in Provence and Beyond
www.picnicsinprovence.com
We provide small select and luxurious gourmet food and wine retreats based at Kathryn's wonderful house. Enjoy amazing cuisine, colourful markets, private vineyards, cooking and sculpting classes, art galleries, relaxed company and much more.

Monclar-de-Quercy

Huit a Huit
More like a neuf a sept. The closest supermarket. Very good butcher and you can buy the biologique bread made by the artisan baker here if you can't find him in town.

Joel's
Joel serves Moules Frites in the Place next to his restaurant and bar. Other times he serves simple country cooking, but the boys' favorite is his pizzas.

Montauban

Ingres Museum
19 Rue de l'Hotel de Ville
Montauban 82000

Quincaillerie Saint Louis
11 Place Prax-Paris
82000 Montauban
One of my favorite hardware stores. I always come back to the States with cabinetry knobs in my suitcases.

Terre Douche
47 rue de la Resistance
Montauban 82000
05 63 66 94 87
Specializing in traditional pottery from all of France.

Zeste
3,Rue Du Doctteur Lacaze
82000 Montauban
05 63 63 18 00
Great flower shop run by Patrice and Thomas Lartet, a father and son team.

Puycelci

My favorite of all the towns, Puycelci is pristine and completely unspoiled. I like the café with the view; it's fine for a croque-monsieur and a beer. It is such a small town that you can walk around it quickly, but there is so much to take in: the perfect church, the houses that have amazing views are all being lovingly restored. There is a pottery that is worth a look.

Acknowledgments

This house was a labour of love. I thank everyone that has been to stay and worked on it and been apart of making so many magical memories for so many of us. With thanks to:

Gary Weis, who even though he wondered why we were buying a house in France when we lived in California, let me have my way.

My brothers, Allister and Robert, for helping with various parts of the restoration.

Louise Fletcher, who stayed many times before having her own house close by. She helped clean the kitchen on one too many occasions, which led my nephew Robin into believing that even the cleaners in Hollywood get Oscars!

The Somersets, Guireys, Pilkingtons, Standings and Coleridges, Gaby Dellal and the Felner boys, Carina Cooper and the Roddam girls and all the other regulars.

Bruce Raben, who gave me the best birthday present ever— a red tractor the same age as me.

In memory of Isabella and Rodney, our cats for 20 years, and Yasmin, my black Arab filly who died way too young. And Greta, Gitana's sister, who posed without prompting for so many photographs. Benoit Belavoine, my neighbor, the person to appear at the door with every vegetable imaginable to welcome us in, a great friend and huge support, was always there at the drop of a hat.

Elyse and Annick Escalette for being the best neighbors ever.

Doug Turshen, David Huang, Jill Cohen and Jon Hugstad for helping me with the design process.

Mel Bordeaux for helping to make sense of my spelling and illegible writing.

To all the great photographers and artists, with special thanks to Tim Beddow for being a neighbor and for having documented La Castellane for so many years.

As always, the Gibbs Smith team, Christopher Robbins, Madge Baird and Melissa Dymock in particular.

Photo Credits

First Edition
15 14 13 12 11   5 4 3 2 1

Text © 2011 Kathryn M. Ireland
Cover photographs © 2011. Front: François Halard; back: Tim Beddow
Photographs not credited on page 223 are by Kathryn M. Ireland

Published by
Gibbs Smith
P.O. Box 667
Layton, Utah 84041

1.800.835.4993 orders
www.gibbs-smith.com

Designed by Doug Turshen with David Huang
Printed and bound in Hong Kong

Gibbs Smith books are printed on paper produced from sustainable
PEFC-certified forest/controlled wood source.
Learn more at www.pefc.org.

Library of Congress Cataloging-in-Publication Data

Ireland, Kathryn M.
   Summers in France / Kathryn M. Ireland. — 1st ed.
       p. cm.
   ISBN 978-1-4236-0672-7
 1. Farmhouses—France—Tarn-et-Garonne—Pictorial works. 2.
Interior decoration—France—Tarn-et-Garonne—Pictorial works. 3.
Ireland, Kathryn M.—Homes and haunts—France—Tarn-et-Garonne. 4.
Farmhouses—Remodeling—France—Tarn-et-Garonne. 5. Interior
decoration—France—Tarn-et-Garonne. 6. Country life—France—Tarn-
et-Garonne. 7. Summer—France—Tarn-et-Garonne. 8. Entertaining—
France—Tarn-et-Garonne. 9. Tarn-et-Garonne (France)—Social life
and customs. 10. Tarn-et-Garonne (France)—Biography. I. Title.
   NA8210.F8I74 2011
   944'.75—dc22
                                                        2010042658